HEART TO HEART PARABLES

Sowing Seeds   ..e, Hope,
Faith   e

Sr. Ave Clark, O.P.
Heart to Heart Ministry
718-428-2471
Pearlbud7@aol.com
www.anextratablespoonoflove.blogspot.com

Rachel Prayer Hour: post abortion syndrome

Elizabeth Ministry: for parents who lost a child

Caring Hearts: for people with PTSD

Samaritan Hearts: for victims of tragic crimes

SOS: for survivors of suicide

Roses: for survivors of abuse/violence/domestic violence

ACOA: for Adult Children of Alcoholics

Caritas: for family with children and adults with disability

Hearts Afire: domestic violence sessions (individual)

Lights in the Darkness: for persons seeking healing from depression

Bereavement Sessions: From the Heart (individual)

Spiritual Direction: Open Your Heart (individual)

Pastoral Prayerline: A Listening Heart

Heart to Heart Prayer Chats: Across the Country

Only the wings of Love and Compassion
can lift and carry us .....

HEART TO HEART PARABLES

Sowing Seeds of Peace, Hope,
Faith and Love

Sr. Ave Clark, O.P.

CONTENTS

DEDICATION

This book is dedicated in thanksgiving for all the gifts our Creator has given to us ever so generously … the birds, the flowers, dogs and even little ants that somehow let us know that the beauty of creation can teach us in humble, quiet, hidden, and unassuming ways to value, cherish, and care for all of life especially by living our Faith courageously and graciously with "Gratitude" of the heart.

"we hold this treasure in earthen vessels…"

PROLOGUE

It takes a skilled story teller like Sister Ave Clark to compose a parable. But when the tale seems to come truly from the heart, and not the head, that is when you know you're in "Sister Ave Land". Her stories are for anyone who has been thrashed to the bottom, stuck in the dark, not believing at that moment that it is even worth trying to get up. By using the humblest creatures of nature as her main characters, Sister Ave exposes the miracle of hope.

Each of her four parables couches a message wrapped in a specific charm. Her little "Dandelion" is particularly for people who become negative about life, believing that everything is insignificant and little, so unimportant in the scheme of vast creation. Here we have the simplest of flowers, finding an appropriate "eternal life" because it has been recognized as a sign of love and has endured. It is a true treasure, valuable according to the Lord's norms, not earthly ones, and so will not end up as trash, but as the permanent gold of heaven. This is a get-down-to-basics story, getting us to wonder honestly, what do we really treasure?

The "Lonely Star", lost and confused, moves on courageously, finding herself propelled along a mysterious path that takes her to a place of even more pain than it had ever known – to a man dying on a Cross with a tear on his face. The sight fills the star with compassion and discovery. It is bathed in that tear, and is transformed, becoming a radiant sign that all who are touched by the pain, love, and the light of the Lord can always share their light with others, together gaining life forever.

The meaning of life's journey is charmingly discovered by the "Dancing Angel" during a visit to Earthland. She comes with gifts of her heart – and the invitation to dance – not knowing how truly these are exactly what the world needs now. This is a playful, but profound parable, another one that touches the heart.

My introduction to the "Bird With Two Broken

Wings" was memorable. I first heard the wounded bird's story in a "live" version, read by the author. Her audience was a group of people who had come to a Saturday workshop on "healing our brokenness" presented by Sister Ave and myself.

It was most appropriate that she had chosen a bird as the central figure for her parable. Birds have long been creatures that stir awe and wonder within us. They are prominent in mythology, and many are the bird symbols in the Judeo-Christian religions. Perhaps because they fly, birds evoke the sense of our connection to the heavens. Or maybe it's because they sing, as Emily Dickinson proposed:

"To hear an oriole sing

may be a common thing –

or a divine..."

Yet, what makes a bird extraordinarily special is its wings. Without wings, they could not soar, would be permanently altered, radically disabled, unable to function normally, misfits, lost, confused, bruised, without hope.

Sister Ave's bird, so free and joyful, flying high, and touching stars, is suddenly catapulted into that altered state. Wings broken, identity shattered, everything lost, the bird must choose to die from despair; or to accept the unwanted, altered state and courageously begin a quest – on strange legs, not wings – to find a new life.

That is the challenge facing all God's creatures who are broken – by pain, accident, illness, trauma and death. And in this lost and altered state, how are they to believe that a "new" life could ever compare to the soaring times of pre-brokenness. Sister Ave's parable convincingly presents the possibilities. Her bird pioneers the path to a new wholeness – a kind of response to God's grace – and is given a prize. In a word – **joy.**

These parables, with their traces of awe, mystery, and imagination, are less about loss, confusion, and brokenness than about belief in the power of the heart, in league with the Lord, to transform that brokenness into a new beauty one could never imagine. I guarantee that all who read "Heart Parables" will by the end have tears on the cheek, a smile on the lips, and a soaring spirit.

Antoinette Bosco

(Author and Friend)

AUTHOR'S NOTE

I love to read a story, a novel, an article or newspaper clipping about life lessons that can be learned. Recently, the news reported how a store clerk allowed a young man who had a disability help him stack items on a shelf. The whole scene was captured on someone's cell phone and it went viral on social media ... a simple act of kindness for all to see. It is like a modern day parable being presented to us ... to share understanding, respect, knowledge and the gift of kind acceptance of one another.

Every time I read a Bible Parable (a story) that Jesus shared, I believe a new lesson is learned and re-learned:

The Good Samaritan...helping a stranger in
need

The Prodigal Son ... a story of how forgiveness
heals

The Parable of the Sower ... how we sow the
good seed of Jesus' message of love

The Parable of the Lamp … let our lives shine
as an example of peace and hope

The Parables in the Bible were Jesus' way of teaching a deeper message of the call to discipleship. In the Parables of Jesus, His visual illustrations touch the very soul of our Faith to become Love, Hope, Peace, and Compassion here on earth …

"thy kingdom come as it is in heaven…"

(Our Father Prayer)

Jesus used ordinary earth stories to provide holy encounters <u>heart to heart</u> … times of forgiveness, shining our light, helping those in need and seeing in the stranger a reflection of God's goodness.

So, I decided to take to writing some modern day parables myself … to illustrate the call of discipleship through a dancing angel's visit to earth, a bird with two broken wings and how he handled the unwanted changes in his life, an Ant named Miss

Charity who wears an apron with a heart on it and a Little Yorkie who once felt discarded and now finds a home and acceptance.

What better way to share the message of Jesus' call to "Love one another ..." Maybe as you engage yourself in the journey of these modern day parables you might just think of writing one of your own.

I hope you smile, ponder, reflect, and share a tear of joy and wonder at the simplicity of the Heart to Heart Parable Stories and find the deeper spiritual message to be one of "Gratitude" for the gifts of Faith, Hope, Peace, and Love that we all have to share .... and become.

(Sr. Ave Clark, O.P.)

"You are the light of the world.

A city built on a hill cannot be hid.

No one after lighting a lamp

puts it under the bushel basket,

but on the lampstand,

and it gives

Light to all."

(Matthew 5:14-15)

THE GIFT OF PARABLES
... A Special Poem

It is night time, the day is almost over

The newness of tomorrow with its changes

and challenges,

Discoveries and disappointments

Will have to wait for the morning sun

A young child is being gently put to bed,

It is time for a story

"Mommy, daddy, tell me a tale, sing me a song, recite me a

poem, teach me a prayer."

Words woven with width and wisdom

Passed down through time

Touch each heart and engage each mind...

Both young and old

Like seeds planted in fertile soil,

They grow and nourish when they take hold

They transform both the teller and the told

When Jesus came to us two thousand years ago,

He was the Word made flesh

The living breathing truth for us to follow

It was a kind of night time then too

He came to fulfill the past and make sense of the future

through His story

But Jesus told stories too

He gave us the gift of the parables

Characters, settings, and themes to show us the way

There are times in our lives when we can see

Ourselves in His parables

Remember the prodigal son who returned home,

Humbled and contrite

Only to be welcomed with open arms

From a forgiving father

We can be that child, or the father,

Or even the loyal questioning son

Then there is the story of the Good Samaritan

We are often called to be like him;

Kind, compassionate

But then there are the days when we are the traveler on the

side of the road

Beaten, broken, praying to be saved

When a stranger, someone different than us,

Comes along to be the answer to our prayer

Then God's grace will flow like the rains

of redemption

A kind of baptism, giving, healing, inspiring

Like the words of Randy Newman, "Right before us,

Signs implore us, help the needy,

Show them the way, human kindness

Is overflowing, and I think it's going to rain today."

Present day parables can teach us too

And sometimes they come from the most humble

And unlikely of places

What is your story?

Tell it, share it

Once upon a time......

By James Palmaro

(James Palmaro, a gifted poet with heart words written in prose. He himself is disabled with blindness and sees the world through his faith-lived.)

THE DANCING ANGEL

All the angels were gathered on one of the beautiful clouds that was to take them on their mission to Earthland. It was almost time to leave when the angels noticed that the little dancing angel had not yet arrived. She was always late ... Dancing ... Dancing ... Dancing ... to tunes of heavenly choirs.

The Creator bid the angels farewell as the cloud moved slowly away ... without the Dancing Angel aboard. Soon after they left, the little dancing angel appeared out of breath and so surprised to see that no one yet was at the cloud called Departure. "Hmmmm," she thought, "is it possible that I am to be the first on board for the trip to Earthland?"

With this thought in mind, the Creator's soft voice spoke, "Little Angel, you were so busy dancing, you missed your cloud ride to Earthland." How disappointed and sad the little angel felt ... she wrapped her rose-colored wings around her sadness.

Her real name was Rosebud, but because she was always dancing, she was better known as the Dancing Angel.

The Creator came and sat down gently next to Rosebud. "Do not worry little angel, you will be given another chance and perhaps it will be a very special mission that will enable you to use your gift of DANCING for others who cannot dance." With these words, the little angel unfolded her rose-colored wings and thanked the Creator for the opportunity to go and visit Earthland.

She did not know then ... but her mission was to be a very challenging, mysterious and a truly gifted mission to treasure forever. Soon a cloud called Gift came to take the Dancing Angel on her mission to Earthland. The little angel waved a farewell to the Creator who touched his heart as the little angel vanished out of sight. "Well," he thought, "what wonderful gifts that little angel will discover and how she will share them and acknowledge them ... that will be her mission for sure!"

The little angel soon arrived at Earthland and jumped off the cloud called Gift. "Good luck little angel," said the cloud, "and here is my gift for you ~~ a sparkling bag. Share the gift with those Earth people who recognize your giftedness." "I wonder," mused the little angel, "what Gift cloud meant and what is in this beautiful sparkling bag." Inside were little hearts of all sizes and colors with smiles on them. "These hearts should be just the gift these Earth people need and want," she thought. "Why else would Gift cloud have given them to me?"

Rosebud set off investigating her new environment. It was rather different … tall buildings, cars called subways that ran under the ground and so many people … rushing, rushing … all so very busy! In fact, what seemed so very strange was that no one noticed the little angel. She wandered in and out of big department stores with beautiful clothes, computers and garden equipment, all with "For Sale" signs on them. The little angel wondered why people were always buying and selling things.

After her first day ... little angel wondered if Gift cloud had left her off at the wrong stop ... no one had welcomed the little angel and no one even seemed to need her. She once again wrapped her rose-colored wings around her sadness as she felt the chill of the evening rather cold and harsh for her fragile nature.

"How shall I deliver these heart gifts," she thought, "when no one sees me?" All of a sudden, the little angel heard a loud noise ... it did not sound like friendly echoes of heavenly joy that she was so used to. She went to see what the noise was ... she was aghast ... a man lay lying on the ground. The little angel helped the man to a bench. He was crying that someone had robbed him and beaten him up. "What does that mean, to rob?" asked the little angel. As he explained, the little angel was shocked and deeply saddened that Earthland was not such a peace-filled place to live ... or even to visit.

Rosebud stayed with the man until he stopped shaking. She walked him to a corner where he felt safe. "Thank you little one. You have a kind heart." That remark made the little angel remember her gift bag. She took out a shining heart and gave it to the man. As he took it … great joy came into his heart and spirit. "Why," he thought, "I feel renewed" and he started dancing … little angel joined in the dance. Soon people gathered around some just watching, others laughing. They asked the man why he was dancing in the street. "Why," he said, "the little angel saved my life and helped me to take heart again." The people looked around and did not see Rosebud. Neither the man or the little angel realized that only those in need see the angel of love hovering ever so near.

As the man danced down the street, the little angel heard the people making unkind remarks … "He must have been hit on the head! How silly he looks dancing around, and imagine, he thinks he saw an angel … now that's quite a story!"

As everyone dispersed, the little angel was left all alone. "What is wrong with Earthland", she thought, "why can't people just dance and be joy filled? What is to be my mission if these people cannot see me?" The little angel had forgotten already ... that the man in need *had* seen her.

The next experience was to be terrifying for the little angel. She saw a huge glow of light burst into the sky. The little angel thought this must be the way earth people celebrate. As the little angel got closer to the light ... she felt intense heat. She also saw big red trucks and people running with hoses. "This is a fire," they yelled, "stand back." As the little angel watched, she saw these brave fire fighters fight the angry flames, carry people out of the burning building and even go up on high ladders to bring people safely to the ground. The little angel ran to a group of people lying on the ground who were moaning in pain. The little angel felt her heart ache. This was the first time she had experienced such pain.

The little angel dug into her gift bag and gave each of the people a heart to soothe their pain-wracked bodies. As they held their hearts their eyes smiled at the little angel. One woman thanked her for showing such compassion. She said, "I cannot get up, but I am dancing inside with thanksgiving for your reassuring companionship." "Why," thought the angel, "I have done nothing." She had forgotten she had given them each a **"heart" gift**.

The bruised people were taken to a big building called a hospital. The little angel decided to follow the people to the hospital. She got on the ambulance and held a lady's burnt hand. The woman's eyes glistened with tears as she whispered, "Thank you for comforting me in my fear." Again, the little angel pondered, "why is it that only the people in need see me?"

As they arrived at the hospital, many people rushed to help all the wounded people. The little angel realized that she was not needed here anymore. "Strange," she thought, "I want to do more on Earth-land but how can I if only the people in need can see me!"

The little angel left the hospital and continued down the street. She was very, very tired and had found nowhere to lay her head. She was also very surprised to see people sleeping on the street in such cold weather. She heard someone call these people homeless people. This also made her ache inside. Her journey to Earthland was certainly not as she had thought or wanted it to be. She had dreamed of beautiful gardens, people celebrating and loving and dancing with joy. Her first day was one of some painfilled encounters, but had the little angel thought more she would have seen the beauty and opportunity of the mission she had been given as a gift ~~ to bring hearts of hope and courage, peace and healing, care and compassion to people in need.

The little angel was looking for some perfect, utopian place. "Perhaps tomorrow," she thought, "I shall do something great." She didn't understand that she already had!! And so, she lay down on the ground next to a homeless man who had made room for the little angel on his torn mattress made of old newspaper. In the morning he made the little angel of cup of hot coffee. She sipped it quietly.

"Well, little angel," the homeless man said, "where have you come from?" Would she dare say Heaven? What would he think? She said, "I just move around a lot." "So do I," he said with a smile, showing many broken teeth. "It sure is one way of seeing the world." "Why," she thought, "the man is truly happy. How could anyone be happy without a home? He hardly has any belongings!" The little angel spent the day chatting with the homeless man. In fact, she felt like dancing. His gentle and sincere smile reminded her of the Creator's smile. "What a fine gift," she mused, "a smile." She asked the homeless man if he would like to see her dance. "Oh yes," he said. He clapped and sang and before she knew it a group of men, women and children (all homeless) were circling around her and dancing too. She gave each of these people a heart called joy.

"What a world this is," she thought as she bid them farewell. They waved their hearts at the little angel. The homeless man just smiled as a tear ran down his cheek. He hadn't danced in years!

As Rosebud made her way up a hill she heard people crying. It seemed like sad whimpers. She peeked around an old church and saw a procession of mourners. Someone had lost a loved one. The little angel got on line and took the hand of a child who was crying big tears. The little girl held tightly on to the angel's hand. At the funeral everyone said goodbye to their loved one who went back to the Creator. "Why," the little angel thought, "they should be happy for their loved one to live in the heavenly kingdom." As the little angel listened, she heard of their affection and feelings of loss for the loved one and how much they would miss the goodness and kindness of this special person, "Why," she thought, "Earthland is only the place where these people journey ... a journey home to heaven and to the Creator's all-embracing love and peace. And what do these earthen people need for the journey but the gifts in the bag ... hearts of joy and hope,

peace and kindness, reconciliation and community …
and love for one another." The little angel gave each
of the people on the procession line a heart. All the
people hugged the angel and thanked her for caring
and understanding their feelings of loss.

As the angel watched the people go to the
cemetery, the little child turned, waved her heart and
blew the angel a kiss, which fell upon a tear on the
angel's face. She too had felt their sorrow deeply.

It was at this moment that the little angel
realized what a special mission the Creator had given
to her … to touch people's hearts, to walk with those
in pain ~~ the wounded and those suffering losses.
The little angel felt her spirit dancing inside at
realizing that the meaning of life's journey is to touch
one another with reverence and respect and give
hope and comfort to persons in distress. "Well,"
thought the little angel, "I guess my mission has been
accomplished." She had only one heart left in the gift
bag. "Who," she thought, "is this little heart for?"

At that moment the little angel was to pass by a prison. "What," she thought, "are all those bars on the window?" She peeked inside to see a young man with his head slumped over on a cot. He was crying silently. "Hello," she whispered from the window. He got up as if he had not heard a friendly voice in a very long time. "Well hello there," he said. "What are you doing at a prison window?" "What is a prison?" asked Rosebud. He looked saddened at her question, thought for a moment and then explained it was a place for people who had committed crimes. "Have you done that?" asked the little angel. "Yes," he said, "I robbed and beat a man to get money for drugs and I wish I could change. I am not happy at what I did to another human being, and prison is a very sad place to be." The little angel looked at her last heart. It sparkled ever so brightly just like the stars in the Creator's garden. She put it through the bars. "Here is a special gift for you, a heart that hopes for new life." As he touched the sparkling heart, a happy feeling went through him. He started to dance in his prison cell and murmur words of hope, reconciliation and healing. Soon everyone in the prison was singing his song of hope. By sharing the hearts, the little angel called Rosebud saw that love and peace and new life can be given to just one person and they will be given an opportunity to share the gift with others. If we help one person to dance back into life, we can transform our world from an earthen world into a heart-caring world, where goodness and kindness shall follow us.

"Ah," thought the little angel as she waved goodbye and listened to the prisoners share their stories of new hope and a new life ... she danced away into the night to meet the cloud called Gift to take her back to her heavenly home. Her mission was completed ~~ or was it?

Just before she got to the cloud called Gift, a woman in a broken wheelchair called out for help to get her back up on the sidewalk and out of the street. "I have no hearts left," thought the little angel as she looked deep into the bag. They were all gone. "How can I help her?" As she thought, she was reminded of the Creator's loving words ... **Love One Another As I Have Loved You.** "Why," she thought, "I have my own Rosebud heart to give away. This means I cannot go back to my heavenly home yet ... I will stay with this woman and journey with her back to the Creator's heart."

As she touched the wheelchair, the woman smiled and said, "Honey, thank you so much for assisting me up onto the curb." "Don't worry," the little angel said, "I shall always be with you." As she said this, a most miraculous and mysterious gift was given to the woman. She got out of her wheelchair. She no longer saw the angel but felt a deep warmth within her heart like a flame of love growing. "Why," thought the woman, "I feel like dancing a dance of thanksgiving and joy." And so, she did and everyone who knew her came and celebrated her new life.

As the Creator looked down, he smiled ... "Well, little angel, you have completed your mission.

You have done a very extraordinary and courageous act ... you have given away your heart so that another may have life to the fullest. What a <u>gift</u> your journey to Earthland has been for you ... for so many in need ... and for all of us in heaven. We rejoice. May your love grow and glow ever so brightly ... <u>dancing</u>, <u>dancing</u> forever."

The woman took her wheelchair to a senior citizen center where she volunteered to make hearts for people in need.

"...a certain Samaritan, as he journeyed, came where he was: and as he saw him, he had compassion on him, and he went to him, and bound up his wounds, pouring oil and wine, and set him on his own beast, and brought him to an inn and took care of him..."

(Luke 10:33-35)

Heart-Reflection Questions:

Have you ever wondered what your <u>mission</u> in life is? How has it changed?

What new challenges does a renewed mission offer to you?

Did someone ever share their heart with you? How?

Have you ever <u>danced</u> with joy, with hope, with compassion?

What does it mean ... to give your heart away?

Write your own Heart-Reflection:

Heart-Prayer:

Creator of Love, grant us the greatness of heart to walk Calvary without a pretense of our humanity -- to ask for help, reassurance and companionship -- to embrace the call to discipleship -- to share one another's burden, and to be Christ incarnate for each other. Amen.

BIRD WITH TWO BROKEN WINGS

It was a truly a wonderful life
soaring above the trees
between the mountains
and gently skimming
the lakes and streams.

It was an adventuresome life
flying from city to city
state to state
and even to foreign countries.
Landing on trees
nesting in backyards
sitting on rooftops
and even in church bell towers.

Flying with friends, strangers
and companions…the bird loved
the freedom, the vistas

that lay ahead with its

changing seasons

of migration and return.

Circling the globe…the bird

learned much about life

in small towns, bustling cities

and even in war-torn countries.

The bird discovered that flying was

Such a freeing and carefree experience.

Perhaps it was the very

energy of soaring to new heights

discovering new trails

that enabled the bird to feel ever so happy,

peace-filled and contented.

All is so often…taken in stride

taken for granted

and just merely accepted

as a constant way of life.

But ahhh…

The bird was to encounter a change

a brutal change…a detour

in the bird's mission…to be

a missionary…an explorer…a pioneer.

Perhaps looking back

the bird might truly hum…

was this the whisper

of the mighty wind?

Was the grounding experience

to be a saving grace?

Perhaps…

But what lay ahead of the bird

was the journey.

The journey of acceptance…

acceptance of pain, change

and a total dislocation

of one's being.

One's dreams, hopes, desires

and most of all

one's security…the space of freedom

dignity, and creativity lost…

and perhaps to be reclaimed

in new ways.

How…hummed the bird,

did this happen to me

and why now?

In the prime of my life…

flying so high in the heavens

and touching so gently the stars.

Beholding the Universe

on one's own wings

was truly an awesome,

holy and happy experience

to end so abruptly

and painfully

beleaguered the bird's drooping spirits.

For he had broken both

of his wings

daring to fly

in a turbulent storm

risking too much

feeling so secure

in the insecurities of life's

devastating and harrowing

experiences.

The bird soared

into a mountain peak

hidden by a fog

plunging the bird

at a devastating speed

to earth

barely surviving…

gasping and grappling

for the energy

to lift one's wings

even just one wing

back into flight.

But alas…the wings were cruelly

broken and torn apart

and felt lifeless.

The bird struggled

to crawl

to a small nook of

comfort and safety

to ride the storm out.

Sunlight…Hope

and a chance to mend

one's wings brought

a very painful discovery
that the bird
would forever remain
wounded…broken…impaired.

What the bird thought…
no more flights
soaring into the
blue skies…and traveling.

What would…could
a bird do
who was grounded?
Birds were made for
flying high above the earth.

Fear…a terrible fear
filled the bird's heart and
his drooping spirit ached
more and more each day.

Try as he could…the wings

felt heavy, lifeless

and sad.

The experience plunged the bird

into a dark space in life…

he hid…isolated and

berated this terrible ordeal.

As time went on

the bird thought…

what am I to do all day long…

and all night long…

die of suffering

or look around this grounded space

and discover

some kind of new mission?

But inside the bird wondered…

what can a bird do…except fly!

So the bird began what was to be

a very surprising, mysterious

and awesome journey…

The bird knew he would attract attention

of the townspeople for…

what bird walked around a town all the time!

But thought the bird

it's all I have left or else I will die

or drift into deep loneliness and despair,

something in the bird's heart

gave wings to hope and courage

resiliency and faith.

So, the bird set out visiting the people places

in life…

Awkward at first…the people and the bird marveled

at his appearances at:

laundromats

delicatessens

bakeries

shopping malls

churches, synagogues and mosques

mental health centers and hospitals.

The bird even went to:

libraries

museums

movie theaters

and even to concerts at the park.

After his first daring and at times

embarrassing encounters at hearing remarks like:

What's that crazy bird up to?

Why doesn't he use his wings?

Look at the silly bird walking around a laundromat!

The bird felt the disdain, mocking and humiliation

of being a wingless bird in flight.

But soon the townspeople were to discover

that the wounded bird only wanted

to feel wanted, cared for and accepted…

Crumbs of food and bird houses were

set up in the strangest of places

welcoming this wounded flyer…to earth.

The bird always longed for his real home

the clouds, the spires, trees and nests.

But

he realized within his own broken heart and

aching spirit

for what could not be…and that he was being given

another chance at life

to find life anew in the misfortunes…in the pain

and also in the courage to survive change, loss

and hardship.

Not easy…for a bird that longed for his

companion birds…

many a tear he wept in solitude.

It was a strange way to embrace

his broken wings

by touching the hearts of the people on earth.

The bird was to learn that very often these

people yearned to fly…

to fly away from life.

At first the bird thought this a

peculiar wish for human beings to want to fly…that

was only for birds!!

But as he listened to their chatter, laughter,

sorrows and sometimes bitterness at the

deli

library

church

school

rehab centers

and on the streets

The bird realized that in some way his broken wings

had been a gift for others.

They saw his disabling condition but they also

saw and felt the bird's determination

to find life in this new disorder.

The bird started to hear people comment

not on his brokenness

but on his ability and tenacity

to steer a new course.

"If that bird can do it, so can I!"

"That bird has guts (he learned that meant courage)."

This made the bird feel affirmed

understood and even respected.

It was the night he spent on the park bench

with the two homeless men…whom he discovered

had not just an extra bottle to share…

but had **compassion** in each other's misfortunes

and even with the bird.

The bird encountered these two homeless men

one lonely evening on his nightly stroll when

all or most of the townspeople were tucked away

in their warm homes (that the bird called nests).

The bird sat next to the two men and listened to their

reminiscing about the past

and of what could have been...

they included the bird as they too had heard

of the bird with the two broken wings...

"Well, little bird," one of the men said...

"you might not be able to fly

but you certainly have gained

the esteem of this town...

you dare to walk among us different,

wounded and courageous

despite your fears."

"Why, we even have heard how

you attend church services

in various holy places...

and hum sweet melodies of peace, hope and

compassion...

now that is a might fine mission."

The bird listened with his heart

and even shed a tear or two.

This made the man touch the bird

with a gentle caress and say:

"You, little bird along with my homeless companion,

are the only ones who have cared enough to cry

with me and for me...

I feel warmed by your tenderness and mercy.

Somehow, I feel encouraged...why,

I do believe, I'll give flight to my life again."

The two men patted the bird a good night gesture

and what would really become of these

two homeless men the bird was not really sure.

What the bird did know was that being grounded

and deprived of what was so much a part

of his life...flying

had brought him to a "sacred space"

of letting go...

and letting God lead the bird with the

two broken wings to an unassuming

and very surprising new ground.

Where the bird would meet the ordinary,

extraordinary, the holy and

the secular and be able to

"look up" and give

flight

to his heart that so much yearned for

as new life.

This new ground was his home...

his nesting place...

Where he would walk among the people

and their broken spirits

and find great gifts

of tenderness, joy and deep peace.

Who ever thought a bird…
who had once soared so sigh…and free
could find contentment
being grounded and surrounded
by humanity.

The daily walks revealed
to the bird all the broken dreams,
lost identities and the struggles
for peace of these worldly creatures.

The bird had found a precious gift
that was no longer his to own…
but rather to give away.

It was the gift of **acceptance** of
whatever space, condition or circumstances
we find ourselves in.
We can learn that in Faith and with Faith

that we will in our brokenness continue on our life's
journey.

Believing…believing greatly in a power
beyond ourselves
that any tears, disappointments,
setbacks and even tragedies
can be turned into joy…
a joy that gives meaning to life.

At the close of this parable…

The bird sets off in a new direction
to visit a refugee center where
people have suffered and
seek healing.
"This is where I shall walk today,"
thought the bird…"and perhaps
I shall give wings to another
broken heart
for this is my mission and it is

grounded…in love

in God's love…eternal love."

And with this thought in mind…the bird looked up

to the heavens to see his flock in flight…and

he did not cry…

he smiled…with deep thanks for

knowing that all of life is a gift.

(I hope as you journeyed with the bird with two broken wings … you were able to identify with some and give wings of hope and joy to your journey and where it has led you thus far.)

"Trust in the Lord at all times and

pour out your hearts before our God

…who is our refuge"

(Psalm 62:6-9)

Heart-Reflection Questions:

How do you embrace the changes that life offers you?

How do you dare to journey through pain, loss and fear to discover meaning?

Have you ever shared deep caring for another person's struggles and found yourself transformed?

When you arrive at the sacred space of acceptance of your life's journey...what gifts of light can you acknowledge?

Are you willing to listen with hearts of compassion to the call to "let go"... and trod a new path called challenge, inspiration and transformation?

Write your own Heart-Reflection:

Heart-Prayer:

Lord of Faith: walk gently with me and surround me with your light…to step into life knowing that Jesus' presence will give wings to my love…this is my hope and my prayer…to remain steadfast in seeking my Lord in my ordinary life. Amen.

THE LONELY STAR'S JOURNEY OF FAITH

The Lonely Star was misshapen and was very blue so she could not take her place in the great galaxy of lights. The Lonely Star had to be content to search for and find her special place to shine … a place where humble people, poor people and very marginalized people dwell. "Where," … she wondered, "was this special place … or did it even exist at all!"

Sometimes the Lonely Little Star longed for total brightness … wishing that she too could be like the Bethlehem Star … a star shining in the darkness and proclaiming great Joy that Jesus is Born! The Lonely Star was to learn some very important and life-long lessons called: authentic love ~~ gratitude ~~ and deep faithfulness … lessons found in the ordinary and occasionally the terrible losses in life that one must sometimes experience to find the light of Faith, Hope and Love. These gifts at the beginning of the Lonely Star's journey did not seem so important ... she took them for granted and they certainly were not made of tangible material goods that the Star's world was so full of.

It was to be a very, very long and hard journey for the star ... sometimes unbearable, at other times quite surprising, perplexing and even awesome. The Lonely Star very often felt like giving up. She wondered if she would have the strength with such a small, flickering light to continue on this journey.

The Lonely Star had no map, no specific role to play ... just a path, an untrodden path to take and believe that it would bring her to a special place where she too could shine for others. Did the Lonely Star have the courage, resiliency or even the nerve to take the path ... one step at a time into loneliness, suffering and sorrow and dare, *dare* to carve out new life, hope and wonder?! Ahh ... so weak, weary, frightened and limited as most stars are despite their brightness, the Lonely Star thought what or who will be her guides. That was to be the Lonely Star's first gift ... <u>to rely on God's Love</u>, the love of a God of great compassion and let this God of insurmountable love lead the Lonely Star through the loneliness and turmoil *but* with a beautiful and sparkling glimmer of what life is all about ... just shining gently, humbly and with great care for hearts that:

    .... give out of pain and anxiety

    .... give out of poverty of spirit

    .... give out of illness and loss

The Lonely Star was able to see at last into the hearts of struggling souls, aching spirits and the anguish of the homeless and violated innocents. The Lonely Star was able to touch, with a gentle light, deep pain and not look for thanks. The Lonely Star was able to embrace the abandoned, the lost and forgotten souls, the addicted, the battered and abused hearts and even the misguided and selfish hearts because the Lonely Star at last saw her reflection in all of humanity ... at last her gift of loneliness was becoming a light of gentleness and respect. All the Lonely Star had was her own pain-filled wish for healing, hope and wholeness ... it was being mysteriously transformed along this path of faithfulness of spirit.

The Lonely Star knew at last the meaning of love ... authentic love, loyal and steadfast love. As the Lonely Star progressed along the winding, twisting and, at times, desolate path of life's misfortunes, she no longer feared or rejected the pain ... rather, she dared to carry it with the gifts called acceptance and comfort; and for this great understanding the Lonely Star discovered gratitude ~~ a deep abiding gratitude. The lonely moments, days, years and dreaded holidays took on a new and real meaning. **Gratitude** for the ability to give ... and not to count the cost. **Gratitude** for the potential to embrace one's suffering and give it a new name ... hope, respect and courage. No cheers ~~ No crowds ~~ No medals ~~ and definitely No glittering lights: strangely the Lonely Star found that the journey of this mysterious path led to a hill ... an awesome hill but not too hard or difficult to climb with these precious gifts of the spirit. What was at the top of the hill, the Lonely Star did not know. All she knew as she climbed the hill and dared to look beyond is that she felt a different kind of peace invading and filling her weary heart. Not a peace free of pain or anxiety but a **peace** that no magic, no power, no money could ever purchase. "What was this peace to be called," she wondered, as she neared the top of the hill called Calvary? She finally reached the top and saw crosses standing in total darkness.

The Lonely Star with her faint but faithful light crept close to this unknown place. The feeling should have been overwhelming and very frightening but something inside the Lonely Star emerged as never before ... a bright and brilliant light ... all consuming!!

She knelt and looked up into the eyes of the dying man called Jesus ... a small blue tear rolled down his face and fell upon the Lonely Star's aching heart. It was in that most precious moment that the

Lonely Star realized that she had been given a precious and mysterious gift called Faithfulness ... the journey to survive and to find life anew.

It was the blue <u>tear</u> of the dying Savior's life that was to emerge as the moment of Resurrection/New Life. The Lonely Star was never to look back to her fears, her anxieties or her heartaches as mistakes, problems, or insurmountable difficulties. She was to arise as the first light of the Easter Dawn called Easter Joy and from that day on the Lonely Star was to be the first flame of Easter Morning called Sunlight ~~ Sunrise ~~ Son of God ~~ Sunshine. Alleluia!

The Lonely Star was to forever shine ... in the hearts and spirits of those who dare to proclaim in the midst of pain, darkness, and disillusionment that Jesus Christ ~~ Son of God ~~ risen from the dead ~~ lives on forever and ever. Truly this was the celebration, to follow the star to Bethlehem and to acknowledge Jesus is Born ... and then, like the Lonely Star, to take life's paths ... and to believe that the Lord will guide and lead us to the glorious moment of dying to self ... on the cross as Jesus did ... to shed a tear, so that another will live with hope and love and great faith. The Lonely Blue Star had been given the <u>tear of compassion</u> at the foot of the cross so that her heart and spirit could shine for others by shedding a humble and faith-filled light of comfort in a world so in need of a small but totally faith-filled light ... called God with us. Alleluia! Alleluia! Alleluia!

May that humble and sometimes lonely light be your strength ~~ your comfort, and most of all ~~ Love Incarnate ~~ in a friend, a stranger and a companion as we journey to our Easter morning ~~ a Resurrection of new life ~~ forever and ever.

The Lonely Little Star found her special place ... it was to be a light to those in need ... to those who carry heavy crosses and search for answers when a little light can shine into their pain ... and they too discover their own inner spirit of peace, love, and profound joy.

As the story ends, the Lonely Blue Star looks down on the homeless and lonely in the streets, singing Alleluia as they receive from her the blue <u>tear of compassion</u>.

Truly out of pain and darkness, fear
and poverty of spirit can be born a
Light … to shine forever called …
Jesus, friend, companion, comforter,
healer. May you see a reflection of
your own journey of struggle, frailties
and surrendering in this small parable
of a Lonely Little Blue Star … for a
great light can shine when we believe
and trust … that the Lord is with us
Always……

"My being proclaims the greatness of the Lord; my spirit finds joy in God my savior. For my Lord has looked upon the servant in her lowliness; All ages to come shall call me blessed."

(Luke 1:39)

Heart-Reflection Questions:

Did you ever have unreal expectations of yourself/others… and even life's circumstances?

What mountain have you climbed … did you believe that somewhere you would find peace, hope and consolation?

What <u>resurrection</u> experience(s) have truly revealed the presence of the <u>HOLY</u> to you?

Has suffering transformed you … given you an opportunity to grow in compassionate living?

What enables you to sing and proclaim the greatness of the Lord … to whisper or murmur an <u>ALLELUIA</u> for taking the untrodden path in life?

Write your own Heart-Reflection:

Heart-Prayer:

Lord, you bring forth the power of justice to all...the lowly, the poor of heart. You stand transformed beside the hardest of hearts and give courage to all the oppressed. I ask for the grace which I am so often searching for...to resurrect time and time again even in my struggles and darkness...to believe greatly that your love embraces all of life and blesses each one of us on the holy journey with compassion. For this I pray through Your name...to bring Christ's healing love to my own soul and to share that gift with others as a Magnificat of joy. Amen.

The Little Dandelion~~Treasured Forever

(A Parable inspired by my friend Arthur)

There was once a gigantic, large green field nestled in a forest of trees of various sizes and shapes of prominence. The forest was the home for many an animal...small creatures of the Lord; squirrels, raccoons, insects (ugg!) birds, butterflies and even some fish and periodically a roaming cat or dog. It was truly a place of God's creative design where even the leaves, berries, flowers and small emerging buds shared the giftedness of their fragrances that made this forest a special, sacred and beautiful place to live. Many visitors came...children, men and women from everywhere to rest, play and perhaps to just find moments of solitude, peace and hope.

It was here in the forest...that the field of green, so green was the grass that one would think it was an emerald blanket of creation so deep, so soft and so quietly exquisite. Many a visitor romped on this field of green playing sports, having picnics or just strolling hand in hand. It was on this field that the little dandelion lived...a bright, bright yellow...a symbol of God's sunlight ever present in the midst of such grandeur. For sure as Gerard Manley Hopkins, S.J. (a poet) wrote:

"The world is charged with the grandeur of God."
So too, was this little dandelion.

On stormy days the forest was unusually very, very quiet letting the rain water its very life of streams, roots, soil and hearts. The tall pines would lift up their boughs and receive this water of life in gratitude. The animals would find refuge in a cave, nook or tree watching the rain bringing new life to its' surrounding home.

The little dandelion would feel the waters beating down on its fragile stalk and lean on the green grass for its protection. After the storm or rain shower the dandelion would appear taller and brighter. It had its special place in this magnificent garden of life. All seemed to live in harmony, respected each other's dignity, uniqueness and connections. It was what one might call...a world of love.

The Little dandelion just always thought and believed this is where I shall dwell forever...but life was to bring changes. Part of the forest had its trees removed and the soil eroded and left a vacancy that no one could fill. The streams were to dry up and some of the fish were removed and saved while others were left to eke out their lives and die.

Some of the animals chatted among themselves of a different life being built in their forest...it was called industry. Was this new technology not taking into consideration that a garden and a forest are places that our world needs to protect, nurture and share with great respect and care. Ahh...no one asked the inhabitants of this tranquil forest what they thought and knew of the beauty and meaning of this holy and sacred place of creation.

And so, bit-by-bit, day-by-day, the noise was not of picnics, children playing games or people strolling; but rather the noise was of bulldozers and concrete buildings and shop after shop called a mall of stores. When all was finished...in place of the trees that had graced the forest with the grandeur of God now stood tall skyscraper buildings called corporations. The emerald green lawn was also being replaced by cement for a multi-tiered parking lot for many cars that smelled of gasoline...the fragrance of industry for sure! All was gone...or was it? There in the midst of this new transformation from forest to metropolitan shopping mall and business industry was a small patch of the green emerald field left as a re-minder...a memorial to the beauty of nature and in that small patch of green the little dandelion still bloomed!

Of course, no one knew of her days and nights of deep sadness, perplexing questions, upsetments and fear. Yes, she had survived, she was saved and she was still living but the little dandelion was alone.

She did not feel the warmth of the surrounding cold concrete and the busy people who passed by in such a hurry (they never noticed the lonely little dandelion) so intent on a new project to make more money. Some even ate their lunch while running from one meeting to another and threw their empty sandwich paper bag on the grounds which one day gathered by the wind hit the little dandelion. She felt the bruises on her fragile and sensitive stem. Why she thought, that never happened in my home when it was the forest of harmony, care and love for one another.

The dandelion pondered her very existence and despite her shining petals she felt deep darkness. What would become of this dandelion she did not know. In fact, she worried a lot about her future and also of her new surroundings. Day in and day out no one seemed to notice the dandelion or the small patch of emerald green grass situated in the midst of this new city life. Until one day an elderly couple stopped for a visit. The little dandelion heard (with her heart of course) the couple chatting. It seemed many, many years ago (in fact well over 40) that this couple had come to the forest for a stroll and remembered the beautiful emerald green grass where they had talked of their future plans. It was here in this forest of life that the man and woman in decades past had carved their initials in a tree surrounded by a carved heart called love. It was in the forest that they shared with each other their dreams and most of all it was on the emerald green field of grass that they looked up at the clear blue sky and promised each other love forever.

Now decades later as husband and wife they returned to the forest changed. "Well honey", the elderly man said, "this place might not be our special forest anymore but it is the very ground we traveled to find and believe in God's plans for us." The woman agreed though she did voice her wish...a wish for the forest of the past back. As she said this the man said: "look, a patch of green...a sign of hope not lost!" The woman knelt down and felt the softness of the patch of green grass and with a tear of memories past she watered its very existence.

The past she realized was the gift that gave hope for newness of life. Just before they left…the couple looked back at the little patch of green. It was then that the man noticed the little dandelion standing so eloquently and resiliently amidst the concrete world built all around it. He went over and said: "Honey wait! I have a gift of love for you." And so, he handed her the precious dandelion. "Take this dandelion," he said, "this beautiful bright flower (it was never called a weed) as a reminder of my love for you forever."

The woman took the dandelion and gave her husband a hug. She held onto the dandelion all day … so tightly that the dandelion felt a bit choked up with emotion and gasping for air at times…needing the soil of earth to live. Where am I going the dandelion wondered? What is to become of me? Do I have any meaning left in life?

That night when the couple got home the dandelion was to listen to their reminiscing about the beautiful forest they once knew and deeply appreciated, loved and respected in their hearts and spirits. (Somehow the dandelion now knew...the forest would live on in their memory). It was then that the dandelion realized that memories are good, holy and helpful ways of <u>treasuring</u> life even when parts of the memories are changed, transplanted or taken away. Now the dandelion did not even have the concrete buildings as companions...and gone forever was her emerald blanket of grass that had been her trusted security where she had peacefully rested her heart and spirit.

Late that evening the woman went into her cozy kitchen to put the lights out. Just before she did that she came over to the little dandelion that she had put into a tall glass of water. She gently touched the dandelion's drooping yellow petals that had wilted during the day's journey in her hand.

She took the dandelion out of the glass of water and her own tears fell upon the petal. She whispered to the little flower (never called a weed) words of gratitude and love (we need to love all of creation) for being a reminder of her love's early years. "Oh," she said, "how blessed I am to have found you. Now I know I have a part of my forest of love to save forever in my special book of memories. I shall press you on one of the pages."

At first this frightened the dandelion…(was she now to be crushed in spirit!?) As the woman said this, she opened up a beautiful book filled with many memories … cards, announcements of weddings, births and engagements. "Here is the page for you, my dear little dandelion. It is a page called treasure. I treasure you …you enabled me to realize today that no matter what changes come into our lives…there will always be a glow of God's sunlight. I saw and felt that today; there you were in the midst of the city bustling all around you … a shining light of sunshine, hope and renewal of spirit. Now you can live on in my heart as a reminder to <u>treasure</u> each moment, every relationship and most of all our love for one another and our world of creation."

Slowly and gently the woman placed the little dandelion on the precious page of her treasured memory book. She put saran wrap over the dandelion so its fragile stem and wilted petals would not be crushed but protected and gently held as memories of joy and love. As she closed the book, the little dandelion did not feel disappointed, displaced or fearful any longer. The little dandelion had a flicker of her yellow petal still intact ... she felt deep thankfulness and joy at knowing it was not being crushed but rather <u>treasured</u>. Its sunlight had served a purpose and found wonderful meaning...to remind others of God's ever abiding presence in all of life is truly a <u>holy treasure</u>.

<u>An extra thought to treasure</u>

Each day...after being placed in the book of treasures the woman would open the book up to her special page where the little dandelion with its flickering yellow petal rested. The woman would gently touch the flower (never called a weed) and whisper: "You are a reminder of love to me...I will <u>treasure</u> you forever."

What a wonderful gift we have to share with each other...the treasure of our love. No matter how fragile, displaced or weary our spirits can get...the gift of God's love can lift us up on wings of prayer and joy-filled hope and enable us to look beyond the materialism and consumerism of our world…to the very heart of our existence to share a simple light of love, to be a petal of bright compassion and a splendid roof of hope to hold us close to life's true meaning … to love one another with harmony, peace, and justice for all.

What a <u>treasure</u>…to see in a tiny little dandelion…the goodness of God and the reflection of Jesus' love in all of life.

"You are the world's light … don't hide
Your light. Let it shine for all;
Let your goodness within glow for all."

(Matthew 5:13-16)

Heart-Reflection Questions:

What do you treasure in life?

Have you ever been up-rooted? How did you feel?

What do you hold most dear to your heart ... as you dare to set your heart not on worldly things?

Write your own Heart-Reflection:

Heart-Prayer:

Let us touch one another with tenderness and reverence. Let us share compassion and hope especially during times of trial and loss. Let us with hearts afire, love the Lord by serving one another with humility and a grace-filled heart that says … "I love you forever … you are a treasure … a gift of God. Amen

THE GIFT OF PARABLES

It is night time, the day is almost over
The newness of tomorrow with its' changes
and challenges,
Discoveries and disappointments
Will have to wait for the morning sun
A young child is being gently put to bed,
It is time for a story
"Mommy, daddy, tell me a tale, sing me a song, recite me
a poem, teach me a prayer."

Words woven with width and wisdom
Passed down through time
Touch each heart and engage each mind…
Both young and old
Like seeds planted in fertile soil,
They grow and nourish when they take hold
They transform both the teller and the told

When Jesus came to us two thousand years ago,
He was the Word made flesh

The liv ng breathing truth for us to follow
It was a kind of night time then too

He came to fulfill the past and make sense of the future through
His story
But Jesus told stories too
He gave us the gift of the parables
Characters, settings, and themes to show us the way

There are times in our ives when we can see
Ourselves in His parables
Remember the prodigal son who returned home,
Humbled and contrite
Only to be welcomed with open arms
From a forgiving father
We can be that child, or the father,
Or even the loyal questioning son

Then there is the story of the Good Samaritan
We are often called to be like him;
Kind, compassionate
But then there are the days when we are the traveler on the side
of the road

Beaten, broken, praying to be saved
When a stranger, someone different than us,
Comes along to be the answer to our prayers

Then God's grace will flow like the rains
of redemption
A kind of baptism, giving, healing, inspiring
Like the words of Randy Newman, "Right before us,
Signs implore us, help the needy,
Show them the way, human kindness
Is overflowing, and I think it's gona rain today."

Present day parables can teach us too
And sometimes they come from the most humble
And unlikely of places
What is your story?
Tell it, share it
Once upon a time……

By James Palmaro

*(James Palmaro, a gifted poet with heart words written in
prose. He himself is disabled with blindness and sees the
world through his faith-lived.)*

Surprise...Two More Parables and Why

All of a sudden ... my pen started to write two more parables; or, perhaps better said, my heart felt a tug to share parable-heart thoughts that speak of those every day friendships and the hidden deeds of kindness and respect one sees exhibited in the goodness of others. Each of these "Surprise Parables" will hopefully call forth from readers a feeling of simple joy, acceptance of the human condition, and a sense of the graces that reside in humble gestures, caring kindnesses and the heart to heart ordinary connections of the spirit.

May the parables of the Little Yorkie and An Ant Named Miss Charity (who wears an apron with a heart on it!) inspire you, the reader, to appreciate the wonderful and ordinary gift of joy that each one of us can celebrate, communicate and share with one another. To see in the gifts of nature and little creatures a catalyst for sharing wisdom, faithfulness of spirit and a deeper appreciation of the connectedness of life ... is truly a lesson the "Surprise Parables" hope to share.

AN ANT NAMED MISS CHARITY

Once upon a time a Little Ant had its ant hill destroyed. It no longer had a home so the little ant wandered around the neighborhood and one day found people at a summertime picnic. "Ahh," thought the little ant, "I will go and see what crumbs I can find." As she neared the picnic table, she heard the people yell "ANTS -- Get the RAID!"

Quickly the little ant scampered under an old piece of wood. She still was wearing her kitchen apron with the heart on it. Thinking she was safe, she peeked around the corner of the old piece of wood only to come face to face with the boy holding the can of RAID. He stopped, looked and called his mother. "Mom," he said, "look...an ant with an apron on!" She told her son to go and put the can of RAID away.

The lady took the ant to a table and put her on a dish of crumbs from the picnic sandwiches. The little ant looked so happy -- she stood up, pointed to the heart on her apron, waved at the lady and said thank you. The lady leaned over and could not believe the little ant was speaking to her ... words of gratitude and thanksgiving for a dish of crumbs.

"What is your name?" the lady asked the ant. "Oh, Miss Charity," the ant replied. The lady smiled and looked around. No one saw that she was talking to an ant. The lady then asked where she lived. The little ant said, "Oh, I have no home, my home was destroyed; but don't worry, I'll find someplace to stay." The lady smiled kindly and asked the little ant if she would like to live with her. "How nice of you to ask me," the ant replied, "where do you live?" The lady said she lived with her son and his wife, their two childen and a dog.

The little ant wondered if the family would want an ant to live with them. She told the lady she would like to live with her and that she would only pick up the crumbs that were on the floor, she would not go on anyone's plate of food. So the lady put the little ant carefully in her purse and took her home with her after the picnic was over.

That evening as the family was watching TV, her son told his wife that he heard his mother talking to someone but when he looked, no one was there. At that moment, the mother came into the room and said that she wanted to tell all of them something very special and she didn't want them to laugh. "What is wrong," asked her son. The lady told everyone to gather around the table and she introduced them to her new friend.

The family watched in wonder as the man's mother took the little ant out of her purse. The little ant stood up on the table and waved at everyone and showed them all her apron with a heart on it. Everyone was quiet as smiles soon appeared on all their faces. Then the lady turned to the little ant and asked her where she got that apron with the heart on it. The little ant told them she made the apron herself from scraps of garments left over from people's garage sales. The family was astonished that the little ant could speak! The little ant then told them that her name was Miss Charity.

The two children, a little boy and little girl, ages 6 and 10, asked Miss Charity if she would like to sleep in their room. "We have empty box tops you could sleep in," they said. This made the little ant feel ever so happy. The father asked her if she was OK with the dog. The little ant said, "if he lets me, I'd like to sit on his head and we could be friends." The big old dog sniffed the little ant. Miss Charity patted his nose and jumped up on his head. They were both so very happy to be friends.

Well, that evening the whole family welcomed Miss Charity into their home. In the next few days, neighbors and friends of the children came to meet the little ant who had a heart on her apron. She sang songs, listened to their conversations, picked up crumbs left so graciously on the floor by her new friends. She always shared her crumbs with the old dog who let her sit on his head.

One day, the little ant saw a spark from a

lighted candle that was left on the kitchen counter hit the curtain that was next to it. The curtain then caught on fire! Feeling very fightened, the little ant scampered to the next room and woke up the mother who was taking a nap. They both ran to the kitchen and safely put the fire out. "Oh Miss Charity," the mother said amidst tears, "I was so careless leaving that candle on … you saved our home." The little ant pointed to the heart on her apron. The mother and little ant hugged each other.

That evening as the family sat around the dinner table, the mother told them all how the little ant had saved their home. They all clapped. The little ant pointed to the heart on her apron, then put her hands together, bowed her head and prayed. Everyone in the family did the same. The father told the little ant and the family that they would all go to church on Sunday together and would pray in thanksgiving for being blessed to have Miss Charity live with them.

The little ant was thrilled to go to church. She

washed and pressed her apron. During the week, she found scraps of old discarded clothing and made hearts for all the people at church. When Sunday arrived, just before they all left for church, the little ant gave the family members and the dog their hearts. They all pinned their hearts on their coats and the dog wore his on his collar.

At church, the pastor welcomed everyone and was surprised to see the dog sitting in the row with the family. He smiled and as he looked closer he saw sitting on the dog's head a little ant who was wearing an apron with a heart on it.

The pastor came over and the family introduced him to Miss Charity. The pastor smiled and asked, "Miss Charity, do you remember me? Many years ago when I first became a pastor we had lots of ants in the backyard. I went out with a bucket of hot water to throw on them. It was there that I met you, an ant wearing an apron with a heart on it!" The little ant smiled and said, "Yes, I remember. You were surprised that I could talk. I asked you to please not throw the hot water on us, that the ants would only stay for one week, would not go into your church or home and also that we would clean up your backyard because we love you. I then pointed to the heart on my apron."

The pastor said, "Now here I am meeting you again. What goodness and kindness are you sharing with this family?" Before she could say anything …

~~the little boy said she helps them with their homework and always says to try your best and to help others.

~~the little girl said she helps our old doggie to feel happy as she sits on his head.

~~the mother said she saved their home from a fire in the kitchen.

~~the father said she reminds them everyday to be thankful for the ordinary things like an ant and for the extraordinary things like an ant wearing an apron with a heart on it.

The pastor smiled and as he looked at Miss Charity he thought of how such a small creature of God can remind us of our call to "Love one another." After the church service, everyone left wearing the heart Miss Charity made for them.

As they drove home that day, Miss Charity smiled knowing her small every day conversations, simple caring actions and kind listening heart-moments meant more to the family than words could express. So she looked at the heart on her apron, bowed her head and prayed:

Be a teaspoon of love…Be a tablespoon of love

Be a gentle heart of gentle compassion

Share unconditional love

Be forgiving … don't count the cost

See Jesus' love everywhere you go

Don't judge … it is so easy

Have an open heart … surprise yourself

Respect differences … find some gifts to share

Share your life … listening with compassion

Walk humbly … with a Gospel heart

When the little ant arrived home with her new family, she watched as they all hugged one another. She jumped up on the old dog's head and he smiled. She thought she heard him whisper *I love you, Miss Charity.* "Oh," she thought, "what a blessing to know and believe that mercy … Jesus' love is in my eyes, my hands and most of all in my heart. As the little ant fell asleep, her hand touched the heart on her apron.

(I hope this simple parable about a little ant named Miss Charity touched your heart and helped you to recognize that our ordinary words, deeds and actions can transform our world for the better.)

"Love one another as I have loved you"

(John 15:12)

Heart-Reflection Questions:

What blessing do you find in your ordinary day?

What surprises do you recognize in your life?

How do you share your goodness?

How is your life full of "charity"?

Write Your Own Heart-Reflection:

Heart-Prayer:

Lord, thank you for the garment of charity to wear and share.   Teach me to be humble and prayerful in my living of the beatitudes. Let me be the bearer of a love that encourages and comforts and becomes a source of peace for all to share.

The Little Yorkie

(This is a short parable about the loving relationship a pet can have with its owner. It is also a reminder that all hearts, even a little yorkie dog's heart, can teach us humans to be extra kind, caring and compassionate.)

"At last," Little Yorkie thought as he heard footsteps coming closer, "maybe today will be the day someone will buy me and give me a home." He and another yorkie were together in a puppy crib with a For Sale sign on it. He heard two adults talking about how cute these yorkies were and then one adult asked the other, "which one do you want?" "Oh no," the Little Yorkie thought, *"please take me!"*

The lady picked up the other yorkie who was jumping and showing his enthusiasm and friendliness. The two adults were so taken with this yorkie that they hardly noticed Little Yorkie looking up at them with his eyes wishing he could jump up and show how much he wanted these people to take him home.

The store owner came over and told the adults to pick one of the puppies soon because the shop will close in fifteen minutes. Little Yorkie kept looking up and even tried to jump but he couldn't … his legs were disabled from being in a puppy mill. The owner told the adults that Little Yorkie had problems and probably will be put down. Sadly, Little Yorkie thought he would never have a home.

All of a sudden the lady picked up Little Yorkie and held him to her heart. He clung to her and smiled his best Yorkie grin. She told her friend that she was taking this Little Yorkie home with her. "He is just as cute as the other puppy and maybe I can help him." She then picked up her cane and left the store smiling and whispered to Little Yorkie, "I am disabled too, maybe we can help each other." Thus began the journey of Little Yorkie's wonderful mission … to be Love …just Love.

The lady and Little Yorkie would take walks together, each of them limping but enjoying their ability to slowly navigate the streets. People would stop and chat and Little Yorkie would hear how the lady had become disabled by an accident. It took one year for her to learn to walk again. Little Yorkie was inspired and despite his own injuries from abuse in the puppy mill, he would learn how to ask the lady to pick him up, put him on a chair and then get him down. Little Yorkie showed the lady that on flat surfaces he was able to trot along and enjoy their walks. She even got him a shirt that says BRAVE that he wore so proudly.

People would come to visit the lady (she was called a counselor) and share some of their sadness and worries. The lady cared so much and listened with compassion. Little Yorkie sat next to her on the chair and looked at these people with their tears. He gave them his compassionate Yorkish grin of Love.

One day, someone said to the lady, "Your Yorkie is very special, I feel his caring." This made Little Yorkie feel that his mission was just to care with lots of Love. WOOF! When the people would leave, the lady prayed for them. Little Yorkie learned that meant she talked to God (who made us all). Then she would pat Little Yorkie and help him off the chair. He knew now he was going to get a treat. He smiled and thought of ways *he* could give comfort. He could listen with compassion and empathy and grin his special Yorkish grin. That would for sure make people smile and laugh.

The lady called Little Yorkie, Mr. Sunshine Yorkie. She told him he was the Sunshine in her life. Little Yorkie thought, "Over fourteen years ago I first clung to this lady hoping to get a good home and I sure did! I am very lucky ... and more than luck I got to be a blessing."

"all creatures great and small praise the Lord."

Little Yorkie Sunshine would now like to speak for himself. So the parable continues.....

One day a neighbor, Frank, came to show the lady his new red convertable car. He was just retired and was so happy to get such a buy. He asked if he could take me, Mr. Sunshine Yorkie, for a ride. "Boy that would be lots of fun," I thought.

The lady put a red helmet on me and Frank put me in the front seat next to him. After I was all settled in the lady said, "Goodbye, I love you Mr. Sunshine." As we drove away I thought how happy I was to be able to bring such joy to people. Frank drove his red convertible up and down the streets with the top down ~~ the wind felt good blowing on my face! I looked up at Frank and smiled my yorkish grin. I could see how much he enjoyed driving his new red car. When we got home, he petted me and said, "You are a special little yorkie. I'm sure glad that I was with the lady when she brought you home." Before I got out, the lady took our picture. She hung it over the kitchen sink and it has been there ever since. The picture frame says 'WOOF' but I say it says 'FRIEND'. My mission to be alive has been a wonderful adventure.

Sometimes the lady says "LEASH" and I know what that means! I cannot contain my joy to go for a walk. Once outside I investigate the beautiful world with its variety of trees, shrubs, parks and even some stores that allow dogs inside. The lady and I have walked so many miles ... and together we have enjoyed each one!

One day the lady took me for a car ride that semed longer than usual. She was very quiet during the ride and every now and then she would pat me and say, "Don't worry, you'll be OK." I wondered why she was worried. Then I started looking at the lady thinking ... "don't worry, you'll be OK." Hmmm, I wonder why we are both saying the same thing to each other? Eventually we arrive at a destination ... the lady carries me into a building. I smell the air and ... GULP! I have an appointment at the vet office!

Again the lady tells me not to worry as she holds me so caringly. I don't like vet visits ...they make me shake. The vet doctor comes out and says... yup... same thing, "Don't worry." But of course I do! He tells the lady to come back in four hours. As the vet doctor carries me to the examination room, I look back and see the lady wave and whisper, "I love you." "Gulp," I think, "what is happening??"

Everyone at the vet office is very nice ... they call me Mr. Sunshine. I shake as they put me in a cage. I hide in a corner and hope the lady who loves me will come back. Soon the vet doctor and his helpers come to examine me. They are very kind and say I am a good boy. I try to smile. They tell me that I have a very good owner ... I say 'YES' inside. Four hours later the lady comes back. When they bring me to her, I stretch out my front paws to hug her ... just like I did the first time I met her. She tells me we are going home now. Yeah! If I could speak I would have sung, "How Great Are You Lord!!"

As she puts me in the car she tells me that I am very BRAVE ~~ I guess that's why I wore my red shirt with the word BRAVE on it! I really didn't think I was brave; I just kept believing the lady would come back and take me home. She told me that I will be on medicine for my little heart. I will have to take a tiny pill that she will crush and put in my food each day. I won't mind that ... I'm just happy to go home!!

Once we get home, the lady puts me on the chair next to her. I hear her pray and then I see her tears ... she's praying for me, her Sunshine Yorkie. I lick her hand and wish I could tell her that she is brave too. She smiles and puts me on her lap. I know she is thinking about the 14 years that the two of us have been brave together.

One day the gas station man asked, "How is Sunshine?" because he did not see me in the car. The lady told him that I am at home resting. On another day, when I am with the lady, I pop up at the window. Then the man says, "Mr. Sunshine, you make my day!" I guess though small in stature (8 ½ pounds) with two disabled back legs and a heart needing medicine, I still have a wonderful happy spirit with a Yorkish grin to share. More than that, I have a special mission ...

Companionship~Friendship~Compassionate Living

All for Love!

(The lady and Sunshine Yorkie continue their journey to be signs of joy, hope, peace and love to all they meet everyday. The lady in the parable is Sister Ave Clark, O.P. who learned as St. Francis of Assisi did … that all creatures praise the Lord.)

Thank you, Mr. Sunshine!

(Special thanks to the best vet a Yorkie could have, Dr. Robert Foley of South Bellmore N.Y. Veterinary Group)

"The Love in me greets the Love in you"
(Namaste)

Heart Reflection Questions:

What is a home?

What makes the home a special place?

How have you been the caring heart of Jesus' Love?

Who in your life has shared with you the sunshine of God's Love?

Write Your Own Heart-Reflection:

Heart Prayer:

You Lord are the sunshine of my life. Thank you for my family, friends, community, neighbors and all little creatures of the Lord that teach us to reverence all of life as a Blessing.

EPILOGUE

I hope as you read and reflect on the Heart to Heart Parables that you take time to ponder the grace-filled message of each one and how it could reshape and renew your life commitment to living the commandment to love ... "to just Love."

...   perhaps in the grace-filled giving away of hearts that the Little Angel from heaven did will gently challenge you to be less selfish ~~ to give so that others have more of life.

...   The Lonely Star discovers resurrection at the foot of the cross ~~ so can we!

...   The Little Yorkie, feeling so accepted just as he was, teaches us to be accepting of our own limitations and that of others.

...   The Bird with Two Broken Wings offers us Hope as he travels the detours of life ~~ detours we all have to embrace.

...   The Dandelion offers us the gift to treasure memories ~~ aaahh so wonderful to hold memories forever in our hearts.

...   The Little Ant named Miss Charity does just what her name says ~~ she lives charity ~~ which is always a gift from the heart. (I hope you get yourself an apron with a heart on it like Miss Charity wore.)

Perhaps you will re-read the parables during the Advent and Lenten seasons, or any season, and find bits of graces for everyday living. It truly was a holy delight to write these creative Heart to Heart Parbles in hopes that the everyday, the simple, and small unassuming events in life will hold graces galore for our living and becoming who we are each called to be ~~ a reflection of the Lord's love here on earth for one another.

ACKNOWLEDGEMENTS

I would like to thank my Dominican sister friend, Sister Alice Byrnes, O.P., for always sharing her interest and support for my humble writings. In each of these Parables is the Dominican gift of "Veritas" of truth to be discovered and celebrated.

To my dear and caring friend, Peg Franco, who is able to read my first scribbles of creating a book. To my friends, Mary Morris and Kathy Sheridan, for doing the final editing and suggestions for placement of the book chapters.

I also thank my dear friend Arthur, who passed away last year, for his interest in my parable stories. He was the first one to say "Sister, you write parables like Jesus does!" Ahhhh, I thought, I must write a Book about my Heart to Heart Parables. Arthur lived courageously with his disability.

I especially want to thank a dear heart to heart assistant, Susan Schwemmer, for being my dedicated typist and late night email sender of chapters to be refined. Her son Eric, great on the computer, was able to navigate us to sites and help get this book of parables to the finished product.

To all my wonderful friends ~~ I cannot thank you enough. You all labored heart to heart and I truly believe everyone became part of each parable ... giving it a life that would relate to others seeking peace and joy, kindness and compassion.

I also wish to thank two wonderful artists – Margaret Lyons from New Jersey and Toni Gasparro from New York for their gracious yes to share their beautiful art work for the Parables. This is their first venture and they both deserve a round of applause!

"I thank my God whenever I think of each of you..."

Sister Ave Clark, O.P. is an Amityville, New York Dominican Sister. She co-ordinates Heart to Heart Ministry. Sister is a retreat presenter and a certified pastoral counselor. She also treasures sharing Heart to Heart Parables ... stories like those of Jesus, that teach us to sow and be the seeds of Peace, Hope, Faith and Love in our world.

OTHER BOOKS BY SR. AVE CLARK, O.P.

Lights in the Darkness

Arthur, Thank You for Being Jesus' Love

(Both are available on Amazon or by contacting

Sr. Ave Clark directly at Pearlbud7@aol.com)

HEART TO HEART PARABLES

Sowing Seeds of Peace, Hope,

Faith and Love

Made in the USA
Columbia, SC
04 December 2018